Life:
a definition
of terms

a book of haiku poetry

Other poetry books by Rachel:

This is How You Know
The Magical Hours*
The Lovely After*

*Available only at www.racheltoalson.com/freebook

To see all the books Rachel has written, please click or visit the link below:
www.racheltoalson.com/store

RACHEL TOALSON

Life:
a definition
of terms

BATLEE
PRESS

Batlee Press
PO Box 591596
San Antonio, TX 78259

Copyright ©2017 by Rachel Toalson
All rights reserved.

No part of this book may be reproduced or transmitted in any form or by any means, electronic or mechanical, including photocopying and recording, or by any information storage and retrieval system, without permission in writing. For information, address Batlee Press, PO Box 591596, San Antonio, TX 78259.

The author appreciates your taking the time to read her work. Please consider leaving a review wherever you bought it, or telling your friends how much you enjoyed it. Both of those help spread the word, which is incredibly important for authors. Thank you for your support.
www.racheltoalson.com

Manufactured in the United States of America

First Edition—2017/Cover designed by Toalson Marketing
www.toalsonmarketing.com

To Ben.
Your support, your love, your very existence is transformational.
R.T.

Introduction

The haiku is a traditional form of poetry that began in thirteenth-century Japan. It originally consisted of three lines and seventeen syllables, but variations have stretched it and condensed it over the years.

While it's changed from its original form—from rather rigid to more fluid—it has not lost its original intent: to magnify a brief moment in time, to illustrate a colorful image, to illuminate and enlighten its reader in the span of a breath.

For the haiku poetry in this book, I have attempted to follow strictly the 5-7-5 rule of syllable count for a three-line haiku. I have also attempted to capture a specific moment in time that, when examined in a broader way, will apply universally to an aspect of humanity—which is why I've called the book *Life: a definition of terms*.

As is always the case with my poetry, I have composed these haikus with one eye on the enlightenment of my readers, one eye on the illumination of deeper truths, and a third eye, if one exists, on the specificity of a moment. So while the poems are short, they are meditations of my heart as I live my life with a partner, with children, and with the greater world at large.

I hope that you will come to see a brighter humanity, a brilliant future, and an unwavering hope in my humble lines.

Accident

It's all fun and games
until one of them gets hurt.
Then it's the ER.

See also: Summer

Adulthood

We like to pretend
we're grown up, but we're really
just kids underneath.

See also: Childhood

Advice

The whole world's working

against you. You might lose. Fight
damn hard anyway.

See also: Bad Advice, Good Advice

Affection

There is a little
boy in my house who loves to
get hugs and kisses.

See also: Bliss

Alive

The moment we stop,
look, notice is a moment
we become alive.

| Life: a definition of terms |

Always

The weekend went by
in a flash of activity
Where is my rest?

See also: Pooped, Years

Advent

The season of
expectation is upon us.
We wait in hope, love.

See also: Christmas with Children

Age

Twenty: I search for

myself. Thirty: I don't care
what you think of me.

See also: Old Age

Alternative

When you have nothing
nice to say, take out a pen
and write it instead.

Amazed

They're amazed by my
grocery bill; I'm amazed
others have done this.

| Life: a definition of terms |

Anger

Sometimes they become
other than who they are in
anger. Just like me.

Anniversary

Thirteen years ago
we joined our lives together
best years of my life.

Annoying

There is nothing in
the world that annoys me like
a practiced whiner.

See also: Days, the Hard Ones

Anxiety, Exhibit A

The air is still,
stuffy inside the house. Walls close
in but not really.

Anxiety, Exhibit B

I can't breathe. My
vision blurs. My head throbs. Welcome
to anxiety.

Anxiety, Exhibit C

It's the fear that gets
me most, dogs my heels, uproots
my garden's flowers.

Anxiety, Exhibit D

Think happy thoughts: it's
not as easy as it sounds
for a mind like mine.

Anxiety, Exhibit E

Anxiety is
not so easy to ignore.
It enjoys notice.

Anxiety, Exhibit F

I've wasted days on
thinking of misfortunes that
never came to pass.

See also: Worrying I, Worrying II, Slip and Slide

Artistic Parents

Working in the late
night hours. This is how you
create as parents.

See also: Entrepreneurs

Arguers

Something I've noticed
is that people who have much
to say know little.

Author

Every book I write
contains pieces of me, my

mark on the wide world.

See also: Know, How to

Awake

Thumps on the stairs mean
kids are coming down ready
for breakfast. Am I?

See also: Saturday Morning

Awkward

Awkward pauses in
the store; once friends, we have
nothing in common now.

Baby Boy

He likes to climb on
my lap, sit and stay for a
while. I don't mind it.

See also: Son

Baby Kisses

The purest thing in
the world is the messy kiss
of a sweet baby.

See also: Bliss

Bad Advice

Do one thing, they say.

| Rachel Toalson |

Only one thing. Well, I can't.
I love too many.

See also: Good Advice

Bad Decision

Stayed up way too late
talking stories, streaming shows—
I'll pay tomorrow.

See also: Artistic Parents

Bad News

The phone rings. The sharp
hatchet falls, somewhere between
my stomach and chest.

See also: Endings

| Life: a definition of terms |

Beautiful

Those boys, they are hard
but they are light and life and
all that's beautiful.

See also: Pooped

Bedtime

As long as he does
not fall asleep before me,
I won't be afraid.

See also: Scaredy-Cat

Beginnings

It's the end of one

year and the beginning of
another, fresh start.

See also: Endings

Belong

The stories we tell
of family give us all
we need to belong.

Birthday

Just another year
older, wiser, stronger and
perhaps lovely still

See also: Old Age, Old Hat

| Life: a definition of terms |

Birthday Party

Madness all around,
kids coming in and out. It's
a birthday party.

See also: Sugar High

Blame

When our fingers point,
when we blame others, the fault's
usually in us.

Bliss

When I'm on the floor
he seeks me out, falls into
a mama's wide love.

See also: Motherhood

Bold

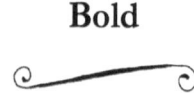

He has lots of words
and he's not afraid to share
them with the whole world.

See also: Children

Book

Each page a study
in thought and speculation—
It is called a book.

See also: Loneliness, Reading Lists

| Life: a definition of terms |

Boring

We take a trip to
see my old haunts, and they're less
than impressed by them.

See also: Reminisce

Boy Advice

Gone searching for bugs,
the ladybug kind. When you
find them: observe. Learn.

Boys, Exhibit A

Always on the move
climbing, standing, racing to
me for one more hug

Boys, Exhibit B

Endless energy
Unmatched curiosity
Billion questions. Boys.

Boys, Exhibit C

Run, run, run, all they
want to do is run. We should
just live at a track.

Brilliant

Planning out summer
reading lists reminds my boys
they want to read now.

| Life: a definition of terms |

Brothers

Let's go outside, play
a little soccer, maybe,
fight—or be best friends.

Business

It's the traction I
need, the traction that eludes
me in my success.

Busy

It always seems like
there's so much to do—even
on a Sabbath week.

See also: Always

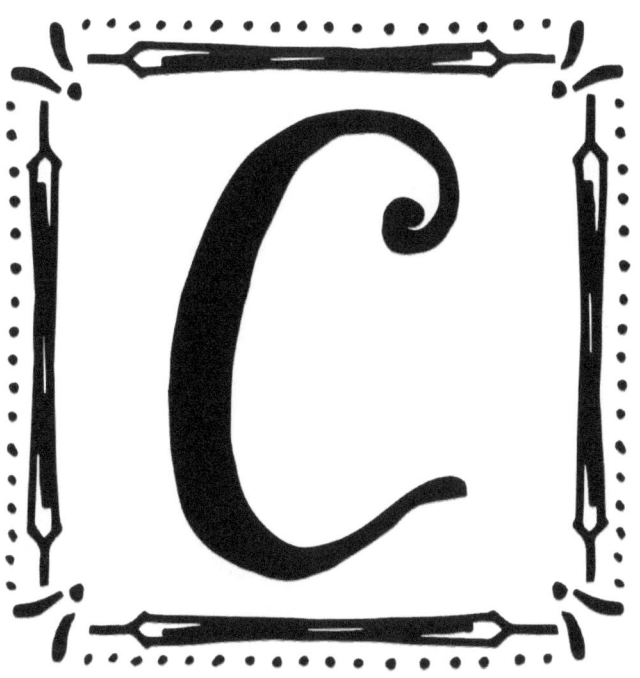

Calm

Music wafts into
the room, whistling, breathing,
bringing relaxation.

See also: Music

Cartoons

They won't go to sleep
because they watched Scooby Doo
and now they're all scared.

Change

I would change them if
I could, but really? I need
only change myself.

Childhood

Crouch beside the door,
a restless shadow. You'll hear
what you need to hear.

See also: Memories, Trauma

Children

They are secure, free.
They haven't yet learned to be
afraid of themselves.

Chores

The every night after
dinner cleanup fight never

gets old—for them.

Christmas Season

Christmas music wafts
in from the living room—it's
the best time of year.

Christmas with Children

They tear through presents,
shriek, play, clap—and another
Christmas flashes past.

Church, Late for

We're running so late
we drive up, push the kids out,
and race down the halls.

See also: Late

Circular

I am weary of
those conversations that go
round and never stop.

Clamor

The hum of nature
is interrupted by the
clamor of mankind.

See also: Environmentalism, Rain

| Life: a definition of terms |

Cloning, a Case for

If there were three of
me, it might be possible
to do everything.

See also: Always, Busy

Clueless

Sometimes what's right in
front of our face is the most
difficult to see.

Comfy Pants

Finding a good book
is like putting on comfy
pants. Everything fits.

See also: Book, Reading Lists

Competent

He likes to pull things
along behind him. It makes
him feel competent.

Compliments

Everywhere we go
people exclaim over our
handsome boys. Agreed.

Confession

Sometimes I wish I
could go back to the time when

| Life: a definition of terms |

I didn't have kids.

See also: Kids, the Gift of; Motherhood

Consequences

A gray square showed up
in my right eye—a blind spot
caused by extreme stress.

See also: Anxiety, Exhibits A-F; Worrying I; Worrying II

Consolation

Success isn't wealth—
at least we tell ourselves this
in order to live.

Contagious

The sound of laughter
is one of life's wonders. It
is pure. Contagious.

Contemplating

I'm supposed to be
reading, but sometimes a day
needs much more thinking.

Contemplation

I could use a space
of time to simply sit and
stare and ponder words.

| Life: a definition of terms |

Contentment

You want everything.
Eventually you learn there's
so much more to life.

See also: Game of Life

Contradiction

Believe—this is where
I fail. Believe? I cannot,
no. But doubt? Easy.

Contrarian

Just because we don't
know what we're doing doesn't
mean we won't do it.

See also: Bad Advice, Rebellion

Convalesce

Reading stories at
the end of a long day is
how I re-center.

See also: Comfy Pants

Conversationalist

You ask him a question;
He goes on and on and
on, never stopping.

| Life: a definition of terms |

Country

What's so great about
country living? The open
wide spaces of things.

Courteous

I will always be
courteous, no matter how
it goes out of style.

Cousins

Cousins stand, eye each
other, then decide to risk
playing together.

See also: Family Moments

Cracks

I'm thankful for my
cracks—they are the places where
the light can beam through.

See also: Tenacity

Creative

Inspiration can
be found in life, in work, and
in every read book.

See also: Book

Creativity, the Truth About

Chocolate helps me think,
so of course I'll need some at
all thinking junctures.

Critics

He says, who would read
the thousands of words you write?
Well. The clever ones.

See also: Author

Curiosity

Curiosity
turns trash to toys, moments to
opportunity.

Daddy Time

Stretched straight on daddy's
back, they watch him turn pages,
sharing a story.

Damage

A lot of damage
can be done in only a
small amount of time.

See also: World, How to Change the; Responsibility

Dance Off

Sometimes all it takes
to make the world bright again
is a good dance off.

See also: Dance Party, Dancing

Dance Party

Dance has a way of
settling the world around us.
Cut loose, let it go.

Dancing

When we have learned to
dance, we can glide through every
twist and turn of life.

Dark

The lights go out, the
secrets come out, because it's

easy in the dark.

Date

What do you want to
do? he says. I don't know, I
say. And on and on.

See also: Dinner Out, Pooped

Date Night

We sat eating some
pizza, talking of life, no
kids interrupting.

Daughter

A daughter's heart is

a fragile thing; like glass, it
must be kept with care.

Days, the Easy Ones

Listen, obey, smile,
play—laughter wraps round the edges
of easy days.

Days, the Hard Ones

When all they want to
do is whine, then all I want
to do is cry. Hard.

See also: Annoying, Parenting

| Life: a definition of terms |

Delightful

He is here reading
a Mother's Day card, smiling
at his own sweet words.

See also: Mother's Day, Part 1; Mother's Day, Part 2; Sons

Detoxification

They stayed the weekend
with grandparents—which means that
Monday's a real blast.

See also: Excruciating

Dinner

We were waiting for

you, Mama, they say, because
no man's left behind.

See also: Family, Family Tradition

Dinner, Complaining About

No one complains when
they ask what's for dinner and
we say it's pizza.

Dinner Out

We make ourselves so
miserable eating pizza
buffet. Happy day.

See also: Date Night

| Life: a definition of terms |

Diplomacy

It's Mama's turn to
pick the music, he says. Which
boy will I appease?

Disappointed

I had to stay home;
they had a fun day, where they
played, laughed, and explored.

See also: Working Mom, Exhibit A-B

Disappointment

Is dinner ready?
they say. No, it's not. Every
thing is late tonight.

Discipline

I know what I should
do, but in the heat of the
moment, it is gone.

Disclaimer

I grew up poor—but
that doesn't mean I don't have
something to offer.

Distractions

Reading books in a
rollicking house is like
decoding tornadoes.

See also: Impossible

Divide and Conquer

Took one to the store,
then stayed home with another
Still quite challenging

Domesticity

We pack up in a
car and paint the town—or at
least run our errands

Dreams

I don't ever want
to give up on my dreams, no
matter their challenge.

See also: Artistic Parents, Dreaming

Dreaming

Talking about our
plans is exhilarating
Bright futures ahead

Dreaming, the Truth About

We must dream for years
in the darkness before we
can act with grandeur.

See also: Dreams

Duplicity

We are all equal: a
nice sentiment, but not
exactly the world's way.

See also: Equality

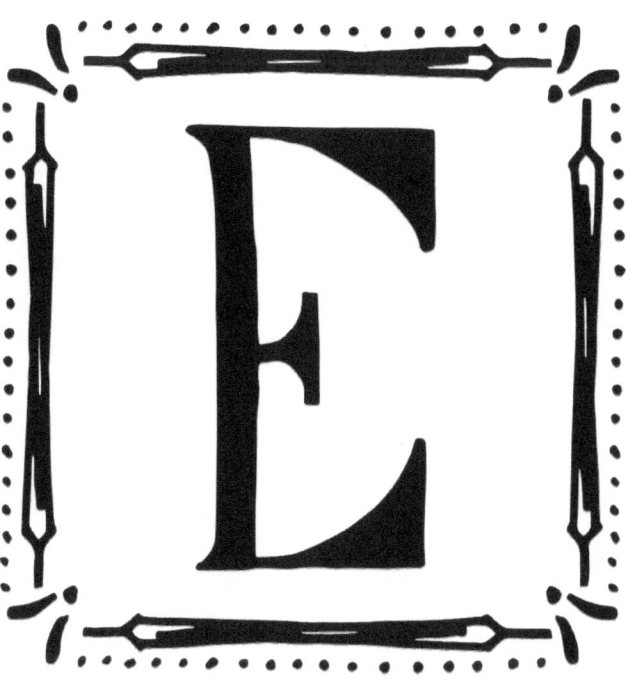

Ear, Lend Me Your

So many words come
my way, so many talking—
I am called Mama.

Egocentric

We grow too comfortable
with our lives, without
considering others.

See also: Selfish

Elementary School

Waiting for a school
ceremony, the noise builds,
a collective roar.

See also: Parental Duties

Embrace

It's true that life's hard.
But I hope we have the strength
to remember all.

See also: Memories

Encouragement

The encouragement
of others is like a sun
in the darkest night.

Endings

We'll watch a closing
door like it's the last one—but
one always opens.

See also: Hope, Exhibits A-B

Entrepreneurial Sacrifices

It's the weekend, but
we work it, because summer
time is slippery.

See also: Working Mom, Exhibits A-B

Entrepreneurs

They watch a movie.

We work. Just for a season.
We'll find our normal.

See also: Artistic Parents

Environmentalism

The earth is not an
unending resource; we must
care for it kindly.

Equality

I will tell you what
I know of equality:
We are not there yet.

Evasion

What are you doing?
I say. Nothing, he says, which
is cause for concern.

See also: Kid Quiet, Twins

Every Morning

It only takes a
few minutes before the fights
begin to break out.

See also: Brothers

Evolution

Many readers don't

love poetry anymore.
They prefer stilted.

See also: Tragic, Writerly Persistence

Excruciating

They're home, detoxing
from a weekend away with
the fun grandparents.

See also: Detoxification, Grandparents

Expectations

Life isn't required
to give us what we
expect—though it'd be nice.

Exploration

Here's a journal, here's
a book, here's a just-folded
shirt. My explorer.

See also: Toddler, Exhibits A-B

Explosion

Patient woman can
bear injustice for a time
Beware her future

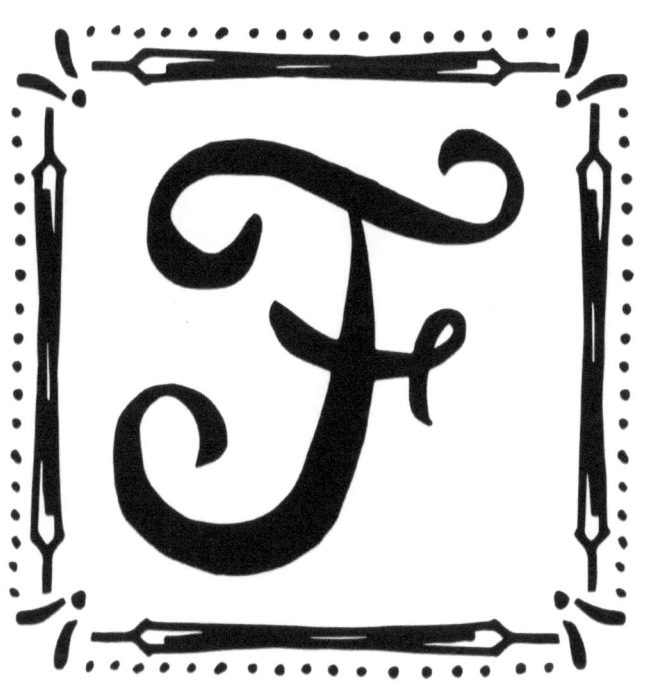

Failure, the Gift of

The first time we fail
our education begins.
Learn from all failures.

Fairy Tale

I am both beauty
and beast, each contained within
an imperfect heart.

See also: Women

Fake It

Act with confidence
and you'll convince them all to
follow what you say.

Family

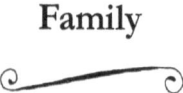

It's a full house, but
some days it doesn't feel like
we're bursting at seams.

See also: Home

Family Matters

We don't always know
what we're trying to say, but
we always know love.

Family Moments

Two sisters and their
husbands sit, play games, talk while

kids watch a movie.

Family Tradition

Singing around our
dinner table because we're
all pretty much weird.

See also: Dinner

Favorite

Fall is a breath of
fresh air, a cool promise of
better days ahead.

See also: Hoping

Favorites

Little books that lead
to snuggly hugs—those are my
absolute favorites.

See also: Magical

Fears

I write about ghosts
and monsters, but the scariest
ones are within.

See also: Anxiety, Exhibits A-F

Feelings

Sometimes I feel I've

| Life: a definition of terms |

become the most boring
person in the whole world.

Feminism

I am a woman
with steely nerves, and soft as
a lover's last kiss.

See also: Woman I, Woman II

Fights, Most Frequent

Technology time
is necessary, I know.
Just not my favorite.

Fight Song

The world wants them to
be different; sometimes I do,
too. Be yourself, boys.

First Son

It's the last night we're
watching a movie with just
him—and I'll miss it.

Flowers

Flowers not only
brighten a day, but they add
color to a life.

| Life: a definition of terms |

Forgetful

I wrote in the books
then promptly forgot my thanks.
That's what anger does.

Found

He looks for me in
a crowded room, smiles, lifts his
hands. I am Mama.

See also: Motherhood

Freedom, Exhibit A

Only five more days
until school starts and freedom
begins in earnest.

Freedom, Exhibit B

Dropped the kids off with
family—now we're going
to sleep for three days.

Freight Train

In times of great stress
I can't control my anxious
thoughts. They run away.

Friday Nights

We shouldn't stay up
so late, we always say, and
yet we seem to still.

See also: Saturday Morning

Frustration

I could not forget
myself while writing today
and my words suffered.

Full

If happiness were
circumstantial, I would need
no more than I have.

See also: Happiness

Game of Life

If you join with me
in a game of your choosing
you will find play. Life.

Games

Imagining clouds
are creatures in a story—
what's more fun than this?

Ghosts

There are people who
live in memory only.
Let them keep living.

Good Advice

Live your life without
turning to the right or left,
straight on your own path.

See also: Bad Advice

Good Day

Eating chocolate
until you're sick—that sounds like
a very good day.

Grandmother

Real courage, she said
is knowing you're beat and doing
it anyway.

| Life: a definition of terms |

Grandparents

Getting them down for
bed after time with grandparents
is exhausting.

See also: Excruciating

Gratitude

Gratitude sometimes
feels hard to find when the day's
wrung me inside out.

Growing Up

Stay with me for a
time and remember all we

have done together.

Gray

Good and evil aren't
so different after all. Two
sides of the same coin.

Hanging Out

He likes to watch, I
like to read, and together
we like to do both.

See also: Marriage

Happiness

We play a game of
Uno, laughing till we cry
It's all in good fun

Hear

If they would just hear
me, if they would just listen.
I'd open the world.

Hear, How to

Listen closely in
the spaces and you will hear
what I'm not saying.

Help

They're wildly weird
today, and it's climbing all
over my last nerve.

See also: Insanity, Parenting

Heroes

We expect too much
of our heroes. They fall down

like everyone else.

Hide and Seek

White bulk on the side
of the couch, watching me. Those
eyes don't let me go.

History

There is no way to
undo what's been done. But there's
a way to let go.

Holidays

It's a day of
Thanksgiving, but so many are
missing. It's lonely.

Home

Take me down to a
place of warm wonder and love,
where I belong. Home.

Homecoming

The hardest part of
returning home is the wild
craziness of kids.

Home, the Heart of

Home is the safest
place—but it's not a place at
all. It's a heart-space.

Honor

Don't forget the ones
who have helped you on your way
You're not here alone

See also: Heroes

Hope, Exhibit A

Lights blink in the next
room, a constant reminder
that light chases dark.

Hope, Exhibit B

It won't always be
this way, he says. I don't know
if he's right. But hope.

Hoping

I am ready to
live in a season of plenty...
any day now.

See also: Dreams

Housekeeping

Cookies baking in
the oven. Don't smell nice, though—
the oven's dirty.

See also: Domesticity

Human

I read to become
a better writer and, too,
a better person.

Hungry

May I have more, please?
Asking that's about all they
do consistently.

Husband, Exhibit A

He loves listening
to Christmas music year round.
Our house is merry.

Husband, Exhibit B

He listens, comforts,
believes, helps, loves, gives. He is
my favorite friend.

Husband, Exhibit C

One look in his eyes
one touch of his hand and I
am pulled back to life.

See also: Man

Husband, a Love Letter to My

A long hug from you
is all I need for the world
to feel right again.

| Life: a definition of terms |

Husband, a Spicy Letter to My

Who is this stealing
into my mind, looking fine?
I see it is you.

Idea

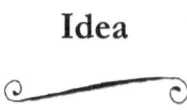

He's digging a hole
out back to bury a time
capsule that won't last.

See also: Help

Ideal

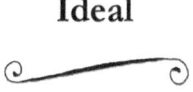

The day was perfect
for traipsing around, reading
a book's lovely truth.

Identity

We all contain some
good and some evil within.
We are all heroes.

See also: Gray, Heroes

Imagination

Stories live in the
back of my mind, waiting to
be turned into books.

See also: Games

Impossible

All I want to do
is read a book—but kids are
climbing up the walls.

See also: Distractions

Impulsivity

He pulls down what he
can find—not considering
the danger it holds.

Inane

The thing I hate most
about lifestyle change is paying
to eat salad.

See also: Good Day

Incessant

They speak, but I catch
only a fraction of what's
said. So. Many. Words.

See also: Not Listening

Insanity

Parenting is hard
most days—and some days it's damn
near impossible.

See also: Help, Kids, Parenting

Insomnia

I'm not sleeping well
lately; too much on my mind.
Exhaustion loves me.

Interesting

Everywhere I go
I'm watching, learning why people
do what they do.

Intimacy

Early morning talks
before the kids wake up—the
story of marriage.

See also: Love, Marriage

Introvert

Today we had a
birthday party, which means I
am done with this day.

Introvert, the Life of

When the answer to
"how many" is "a bunch," then
I'd rather stay home.

Ironic

We're away from the
kids, so what do we do? We
watch their videos.

Irony

Once I did not like
to clean. Now I know it holds
my best ideas.

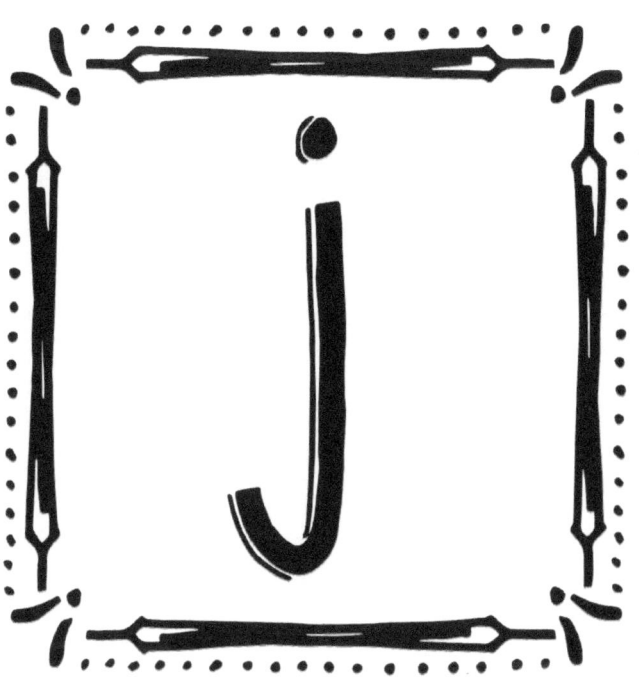

Jealous Thought

A jealous thought can
grow and grow 'til you can't see
yourself anymore.

Jealousy

Jealousy is just
a symptom of persistent
insecurity.

Jealousy, Advice on

Let not jealousy
tell you who you must be. It
doesn't know enough.

Jingle

Rain, rain, go away,
please don't make a mom insane.
(Boys need the outdoors.)

See also: Help

Judgment

I left hastily.
But I can't stand sharing a
room with cold judgment.

See also: Family Matters

Justification

Stop gritting your teeth,

| Life: a definition of terms |

the dentist says. I live with
seven males, I say.

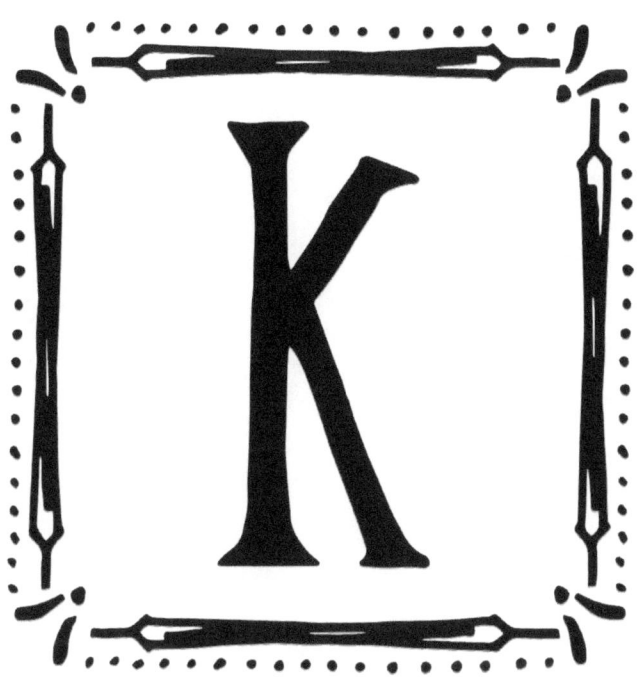

Kidless Days

Days without the kids
move slowly, quietly—we
can hear ourselves think.

Kid Quiet

The only time they're
quiet is when they're drawing,
reading, or sleeping.

Kids

They tattle, they fight,
they drive me up one wall and
down another. Kids.

Kids, the Gift of

Sunshine and laughter—
this is what we miss of life
when kids don't exist.

See also: Confession, Motherhood

Kids, the Growing Up of

You don't notice time
passing until you see how
they've all grown older.

Know, How to

If you want to know
who I am, all you have to
do is read my books.

| Life: a definition of terms |

See also: Author

Last Baby

Little curls at the
nape of his neck tickle his
ears. He is lovely.

See also: Bliss, Motherhood

Late

Chilly morning, they
scramble for jackets, we run
on the way to school.

See also: Freedom, Exhibit A

Lazy Saturday

It's just a lazy

Saturday, at the end of
which nothing is done.

Learn

We learn from reading,
whether we know it or not.
Stories shape our lives.

See also: Human

Lessons

I left the bathroom
door open, so he comes to
explore. Lesson learned.

Library

The library is
a magical place for a
child. Even grown ones.

Life

Another day gone
work, sleep, love, and before you
know it, it's over.

Life Lessons

You take for granted
all the things that go right—least
until they go wrong.

See also: Trauma

Life, the Story of My

Such a longing in
me to do more, be more. At
times it overwhelms.

Lifetime

It's been a long day
in a quick life with years that
flash by in a blur.

Lights

I don't turn off lights
in my house at night. Horrors
live in the darkness.

See also: Bedtime, Scaredy-Cat, Scary

Listen

Silence often says
what our words cannot, filling
the empty spaces.

Loneliness

A good book is a
fantastic cure for the old
vice of loneliness.

See also: Book

Lost in Translation

It sounds perfect in

my head. But somehow it gets
lost in translation.

Love

Love shows up gently
in bodies and words—softly,
unannounced, startling.

Love and Marriage

The steps aren't always
perfect, but the dance turns out
all right in the end.

See also: Love

| Life: a definition of terms |

Loved

Gathering flowers
on a fresh spring day, they bring
them all to Mama.

Lovely

Laughter of brothers
is one of the loveliest
sounds a mom can hear.

Lover

You lie beside me,
your arm brushing mine and there
is nothing better.

See also: Husband, Exhibits A-C

Love Story

It is a story
of love, passion, and knowing—
this story with you.

Lullaby

Voices rising, then
falling in a rhythm that
walks the way to sleep

Magical

My favorite time with
children is the magical
hour of stories.

Man

There is a great man
living, largely, in my home
I call him husband

See also: Husband, Exhibits A-C

Manners, the Changing of

If we want children
to learn good manners today,
we'll have to teach them.

Marketing, My Relationship with

I don't like to sing
my own praises. There's enough
of that in the world.

Marriage

Crammed on a love seat
sinking closer together
we work but connect

Marriage Cycles

We fight, we make up,
we fight again, both imperfect
people, married.

Mask

How are you? Just fine.
Got my mask in place, grin and
bear it, no one sees.

Melody

Sometimes there are words
that can only be conveyed
through a melody.

See also: Music

Memories

I only recall
snippets of my childhood
mostly the warm ones

Memory

The memory fades,
but there are photographs to
remind, to record.

Mess

The world my children
will inherit is not one
I would like to have.

See also: Environmentalism

Mind

I know I could save
hours by not worrying…

have you met my mind?

See also: Anxiety, Exhibits A-F

Mindreading

They keep asking when
he'll be here, but I don't know
the plans of others.

Missing

Where is my sense of
adventure? I fear I
traded it for routine.

See also: Feelings

Missing Out

Today I shop for
Christmas while everyone else
decorates the tree.

Mistakes, the Truth About

Not all advice is
beneficial. Some prevents
valuable mistakes.

See also: Good Advice

Modernity

On my back deck, life's
modern conveniences drown
out nature's sweet song.

Monsters

That thing at the top
of the stairs is worse when you're
walking them alone.

See also: Lights, Terrors

Mornings

I wanted to stay
in bed. But I'm a mom, which
means I must get up.

Motherhood

It is in motherhood
that I have most learned to

love well and be loved.

See also: Delightful, Sons

Mother's Day, Part 1

Stay in bed, the note
says. They bring breakfast and a
movie they made me.

Mother's Day, Part 2

They walk in the door
and shower me with cards, gifts,
flowers, hugs. Their love.

See also: Delightful

| Life: a definition of terms |

Movie Night

Everyone gathered
to watch a movie. Quiet
for a few hours.

Music

The piano keys
fill our house with music; their
voices rise, meet it.

My Father

I tried to write you
a poem but couldn't find
words for the leaving

See also: Sorrow, Tenacity

Mysteries

What do you want from
me? I wish I knew; some things
remain mysteries.

Nature

Go out into the
beauty of nature and learn
a little something.

See also: Boy Advice

Nature, the Beauty of

Often I sit on
my back porch, reading, my heart
broken by beauty.

Never Again

I took them all school
shopping today and I'm still
feeling half-crazy.

See also: Lessons

New Year

The new year begins
with fanfare, but the quiet
moments pave its way.

Night Terrors

I pull the covers
over my head so the night
terrors can't see me.

See also: Lights, Scaredy-Cat, Terrors

Nonstop

He talks about stop
motion films. Remarkable,
but so many words.

See also: Incessant

Note

If I could say one
thing to you, it would be this:
You are beloved.

Notebook

Everything I do,
everywhere I go, I am
collecting stories.

See also: Observer

Not Listening

He talks nonstop of
Minecraft; I find attention
quite hard to give him.

See also: Incessant, Nonstop

Observation

Mechanization
only makes things faster, not
actually better.

Observer

I am a writer,
which means I watch, constantly,
what you say and do.

See also: Notebook

Offering

The art I offer
is my interpretation
of a wounded world.

Old Age

Wisdom is the crown
of age. So every year I
grow older, wiser.

See also: Birthday

Old Hat

The thing 'bout getting
older: you'll spot a mistake
from miles away.

Opposing Forces

I'm trying to think,
they're trying to talk; someone

won't get what they want.

See also: Impossible

Others

We are afraid of
those we don't know, but they're the
ones who teach us most.

Overwhelmed

Feeling overwhelmed
makes me want to quit doing
everything, curl up.

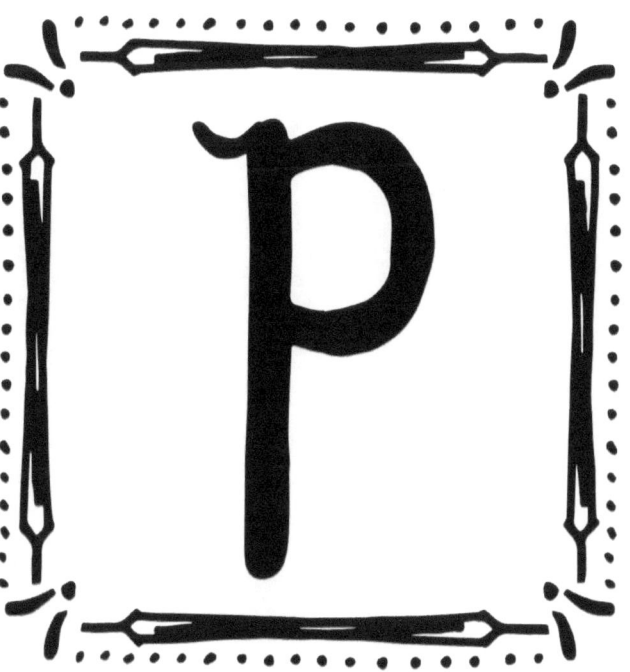

Panic

Scrambling madly to
clean up my house before all
my guests come over.

See also: Cloning, a Case for

Paradox

When they're acting fools
it's both maddening and
mildly hilarious.

See also: Kids

Paradoxical

My thoughts about a

new year are, by turns, hopeful,
grand, and despairing.

Parental Duties

Another award
ceremony in the books.
It's the end of school.

See also: Elementary School

Parenting

Sometimes you're so done
you can't take another word
or question or kiss.

See also: Help

Parenthood, Exhibit A

What does a mother
give to her children? Life. But
also her own life.

Parenthood, Exhibit B

What does a father
give to his children? Love, play,
and identity.

Past

Memories live in
the looking back. I don't want
to ever forget.

See also: Ghosts

Perseverance

If we keep going,
if we never give up, we'll
see the tide turn good.

Persistence

Even if it goes
nowhere the first time, you try,
try, and try again.

See also: Tenacity

Perspective

Seeing the world through
the lens of a camera

changes perspectives.

Phone Addiction

It's a bad habit,
he says, pocketing his phone.
So break it, I say.

Phone Culture

Turn off your phone, she
said. Just a sec, he said. So
she is forgotten.

See also: Phone Addiction

Photo Art

She cocks her head, asks

what is it? A true photo
need not be explained.

Photographs

Where is it we live
most? In our photographs, stuffed
in pockets of books.

See also: Memory

Photography

Viewing life through a
lens is sometimes all we need
to see it anew.

See also: Perspective

Platitude

The world will bring you
to your knees, son, but you must
not give up. Ever.

See also: Perseverance

Play

Running around a
playground, we pretend to be
chased by dinosaurs.

Pleasurable

Simple pleasures: like
an air conditioner that
works in the summer.

Pooped

Such exhaustion did
not exist until kids were
welcomed to my life.

See also: Zoo

Popcorn

A bowl of popcorn
gets us through the days we don't
want to eat healthy.

Possibility

It's possible to
do, be anything if we

know ourselves and work.

Potter, Beatrix

Beatrix Potter
still appeals today like she
did back in her day.

Power

Kids who love stories
are kids who embrace a whole
lifetime of learning.

Practice

Practice makes perfect—
but only the right kind of
purposeful practice.

Prank

They have drawn with chalk
on every deck chair, so my
backside's a portrait.

See also: Sons

Preferences

I like what I like
and dislike what I dislike
with great vehemence.

Present

Today I try to
notice everything about

them, watching, loving.

See also: Time, Years

Pretend

Caught him reading a
book, cover to cover, though
he does not know how.

Procrastination

I have all this time
to write a brilliant poem—
and I put it off.

Productivity

Driving all morning,

then organizing—it's been
a productive day.

Promise

I can feel what it
does to me when you are gone
Please be here always

See also: Lover

Proverb

A man who cannot
examine his past is a
man who goes nowhere.

Punctual

Running late is not
something I enjoy doing.
I prefer on time.

Pursuit of Happiness

Happiness is found
in what we want but don't have,
for life's a pursuit.

Queen

I am the queen of my castle, but it is a messy, smelly one.

Question

What can you tell me about everything in the world? my children ask.

See also: Curiosity

Rain

Face the rain. Smell its
wet. Look up. Discover the
glorious rainbow.

Read

I read so that I
can write better, more
imaginative stories.

Reading Lists

There are so many
good books to read, so many
new worlds to explore.

See also: Convalescence

Reality

Sometimes what the day
holds is not great learning, but
terrible surprise.

See also: Bad News

Rebellion

You can't do it that
way, they say, to which I reply—
well, now, watch me.

See also: Bad Advice

Recuperate

At the end of a
long day, all I really want
is to read a book.

See also: Magical

Regret

Maybe we'll always
regret something. Maybe we
regret the right thing.

Rejection

Rejection sometimes
feels like a commentary
on worth, but it's not.

Relationships

The measure of a
relationship happens in
the silent spaces.

Relentless

I want to be so
relentless the world can't help
but be changed for good.

Reminisce

A campground, railroad
tracks, a running track—we see
them all and go home.

Resistant

You should read this, I
say. Just a minute, he says.
Never a good time.

See also: Phone Addiction

Resolve

I will defy the
odds. I will survive. Life won't
win so easily.

Responsibility

Life should be lived in
such a way that others are
hastened back to life.

See also: World, How to Change the

Ridiculous

I finally have
a stretch of time to read and
I spend it cleaning.

Romance

A life lived without
romance is, indeed, not much
of a life at all.

Routine

Often, the details
of daily life seem mundane.

They hold happiness.

Rule-breakers

They jump rope in the
house, which makes me want to trip
them up and then laugh.

Running Late

Waiting in the car
for those who should be with me—
story of my life

Running, the Delight of

Running, breathless, we
laugh at the sound of pounding
feet. The race is on.

Saturday Morning

It's Saturday morning
They knock on our door, ask
"When's breakfast coming?"

See also: Expectations

Scare

This can't happen to
me. That's the first thought. And then:
how will I survive?

See also: Bad News

Scaredy-Cat

I do not delight

in what I fear; I run from
every last monster.

See also: Bedtime, Lights

Scary

We watch "Stranger Things"
and I can't be in a room
alone anymore.

See also: Lights

School

Summer has done a
number on me—I'm ready
for restoration.

See also: Freedom, Exhibit A

Secrets

We think protection
is best, but indefinite
doubt just frightens kids.

Selfish

We are only a
small part of the world. We act
like the only part.

See also: Egocentric

Shake it Off

The election's done,
the day is gray, but a flower
blooms in the yard.

Sharing

We are listening
to a story—me sewing,
them building LEGOs.

Shopping

Everything takes twice
as long when you bring with you
a parcel of kids.

See also: Never Again

Shows

We stay up too late
catching up on "Game of Thrones."

Yeah, we're addicted.

See also: Friday Nights

Shower

Water rolling in
beads all over the surface
of skin. I am clean.

Simplicity

They don't need to go
glamorous places. They just
need a craft table.

See also: Children

Singing

Singing lifts a weary
spirit so it can soar
to the greatest heights.

Sister, Exhibit A

A sister knows you
inside out and can only
shake her head and love.

Sister, Exhibit B

A sister is a
friend who cannot turn her back.
Where she goes, I go.

| Life: a definition of terms |

Sister, Exhibit C

A sister is a
friend, confidante, a sweet gift
I have a good one

See also: Sister Times

Sisters

You know what I don't
say, no matter how long it's
been. We are sisters.

Sister Times

Some of the best times
in my life were spent with a
sweet, loving sister.

Sit, How to

We eat dinner at
the same table every night
and still they're confused.

See also: Kids

Slackers

Instead of doing
what needs done, we sit down and
sing—like the old days.

Slap Bracelets

The only thing slap
bracelets are good for is kids

fighting over them.

Sleepless

Anxiety bites
at the base of my throat, makes
it so hard to sleep.

See also: Insomnia

Slip and Slide

Mental health is a
slippery thing—fine today,
a mess tomorrow.

Sneaky

He climbs in our bed

for some quiet moments on
Saturday morning.

Son

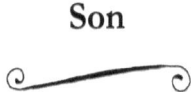

He looks at me with
the blue eyes his daddy gave
him. We exchange love.

Sons

They share as brothers
share: ideas, plans, fun. They
teach me how to be.

See also: Motherhood

| Life: a definition of terms |

Sorrow

Unspeakable pain
has a way of remaking
us if we let it.

Sounds

The clicking of keys
the snapping of photos—the
sounds of conference.

Soundtrack, Exhibit A

Weaving in and out
of rooms, days, moments, is their
humming song of life.

Soundtrack, Exhibit B

We listen to music
like it's the soundtrack of
our lives. Well, it is.

Speeches

Give me a notebook
and words flow; give me a
microphone and they don't.

Spring Break

The one weekend we
go to the country, it rains
every single day.

Springtime

Springtime comes in a
million different shades, colors,
and with it comes hope.

Statue

The lion sits on
the words of history as
if it understands.

Stranger

If you don't read my
writing, you probably won't
know me well at all.

See also: Author; Know, How to

Strong-willed

He doesn't ever
ever quit, which is great unless
you're his parent.

Stuck

The best way to feel
stuck is to believe there's no
other solution.

Students

What is the subject
you would like to learn today?
All of them, they say.

Sugar High

Laugh, laugh, cry, cry, laugh,
cry, the emotional turns
of a sugar high.

See also: Birthday Party

Summer I

Summer unfolds hot
and endless, it seems, but it's
gone way, way too soon.

Summer II

Summer forgets its
structure, in favor of long,
lazy, fluid days.

Summer III

Summer likes to play
games on the floor, do puzzles,
and most of all read.

Summer IV

Summer has a quite
distinct volume about it:
loud, louder, loudest.

Summer V

Summer offers days
of building amazing things
on a LEGO mat.

Summer VI

Summer spreads its mess
all over the house, and I
can't keep up with it.

Summer VII

Summer spins in a
circle round boys who crave
freedom, fun, family.

Summer VIII

Summer gives us sun,
smiles, sandwiches on blankets,
spread on a park's ground.

Summer IX

Summer is mostly
loud living, constant fights, and
wild activity.

Summer X

Fighting, constantly
One takes a swing, one screams, you
gotta love summer.

Summer XI

Summer is also
laughter shaking at the edge
of our memories.

See also: School

| Life: a definition of terms |

Summertime Blues

Summer's destroying
my hard-working schedule; can't
get much done these days.

Sunny Day

Perfection in a
day is hard to come by. When
it does, I choose play.

See also: Play

Superheroes, Exhibit A

Superheroes fly
on the road to school, their capes

flapping in the wind.

Superheroes, Exhibit B

They want to wear their
costumes everywhere. Batman
guards me at the store.

See also: Boys, Exhibits A-C

Surprise

In the span of a
dinner your whole life can change
irrevocably.

Sweet

We watch a movie

together for once, no one
working, just being.

Swimming

Headed to the pool
because it's the best place for
six water monsters.

See also: Sunny Day

Sympathy

There's only so much
I can take, I said. Well, he
said. People are dumb.

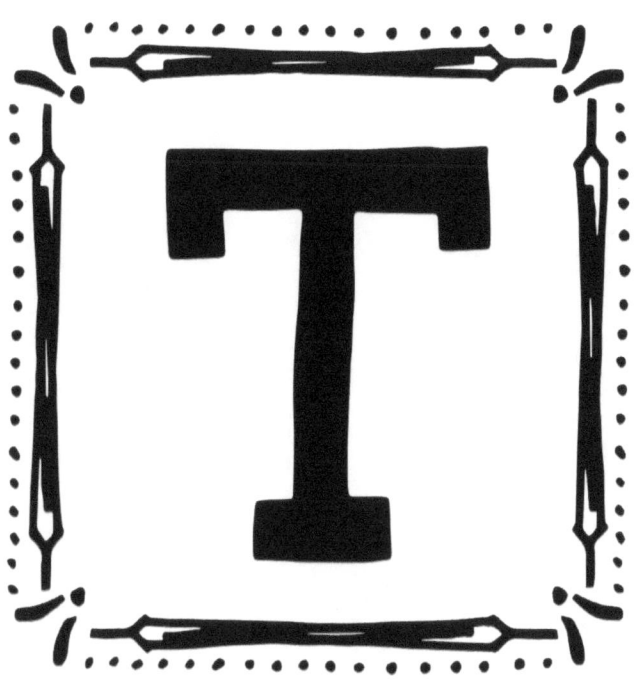

Talkative

He wakes up talking,
he goes to bed talking. He's
forever talking.

See also: Incessant, Not Listening, Nonstop

Teachers

All my old English
teachers showed up at a book
signing—so special.

Temper

We temper our red
temper, but it's either a
blade out or one in.

Tenacity

I've been knocked down a
time or two, but I've always
gotten right back up.

See also: Perseverance

Terror

We are woken up
at 2:30 a.m. by
pounding feet of twins.

Terrors

When the eve is young
the terrors seem far away

Dark brings them flying.

See also: Lights, Monsters

Thunderstorm

The rumbling of a
thunderstorm is nature's call
to wake and enjoy.

Time

I can't grasp the years,
though the days stretch long; time's a
shadow left behind.

See also: Years

Timeless

The stories that are
timeless are the best ones to
keep in libraries.

Time, Notes on

Time moves silently.
We only note its passing
in aging faces.

See also: Kids, the Growing Up of

Toddler, Exhibit A

I'm doing laundry,
he's following me around
helping—not really.

| Life: a definition of terms |

Toddler, Exhibit B

Fill it up, push it,
trip, fall, return to the one
who kisses hurts gone.

Tragic

We do not walk in
freedom so much as we walk
chained to familiar.

See also: Evolution

Transformation

Echo into the
farthest corners of the world

and then just listen.

Transient

Never-ending, that's
the way it feels some days, though
I know it will end.

See also: Time

Trauma

The calm before the
storm is always the scariest
part of trauma.

| Life: a definition of terms |

Traveling

Stuck in a car with
wild monkeys is not my
favorite thing to be.

Trip

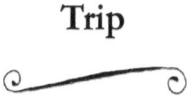

Going anywhere
with boys requires so much
preparation time.

Truth for Everyone

Don't know what drives a
man to kill another. Do
know we are all loved.

See also: Note

Try

When we reach the end
of our possibility
we just try again.

Twins

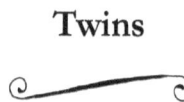

The constant demand
for vigilance is what wrecks
me most—there's no rest.

See also: Terror

Twins, the Truth About

One has the same face
as another and yet they

are very different.

Under the Bed

Something lives beneath
my bed. It's called my own dark
imagination.

See also: Bedtime, Scaredy-Cat

Uninterrupted

We sleep a little
too late when there are no kids
to shake us awake.

See also: Kidless Days, Lazy Saturday

Unity

We are all the same

deep down inside. Genius finds
threads of unity.

Unknowable

Even if one heart
walks in step with another
it is still unknown.

Unproductive

A day off from school
means that not a whole lot of
work gets done either.

See also: Working Mom, Exhibits A-B

Unvacation

All day without kids
was not enough, because I
didn't get to rest.

Useless

They're sorting Legos
into colors. Five minutes
later they give up.

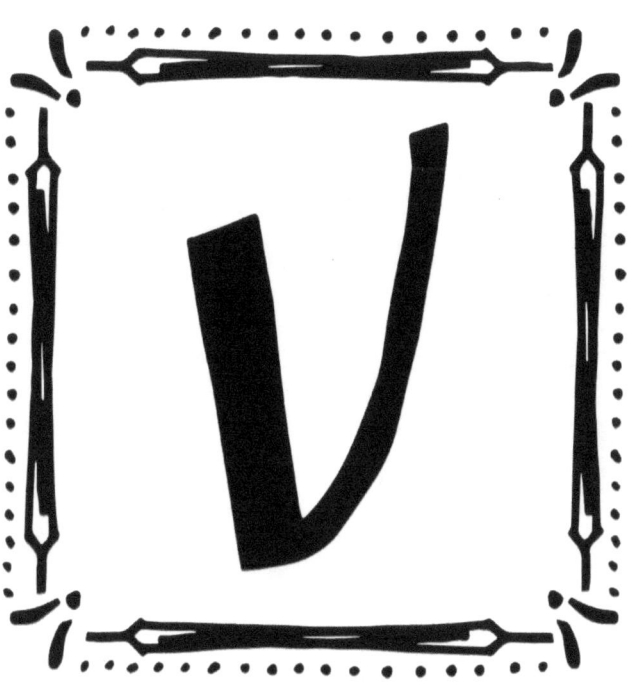

Vacation

Summer is closing
down—some days too fast, some days
not quite fast enough.

Walls, Bouncing Off the

They are wired from
a birthday party. Will we
ever get to bed?

See also: Sugar High

Want

Mentioning silence
to a parent's like pointing
out impossibles.

Wellness

We will our bodies
to heal. We tell them what to
do, and they do it.

Well Read

To be well read is,
perhaps, the greatest
accomplishment in a life.

See also: Power

Whirlwind

Another day,
another night, time doesn't slow
for those who may ask.

See also: Time

Whoops

The worst kind of
conversation's the one you thought
you had—but didn't.

Wild Ride

It is amazing
how one can go from calm to
crazy in no time.

Wind

A wind blows gently
and yet can stir the deepest
waters from their calm.

Wishes

I wish I could eat
pizza every day and keep
a decent figure.

See also: Good Day

Wishing vs. Worrying

I spend half my life
wishing I had more time to
read, write, and eat pie.

I spend the other
half of my life worrying
about what's coming.

Women

All the women in
me are imperfect, unjust,
but still becoming.

Woman I

I am a woman.
I do not apologize
for who I am. No.

Woman II

They say we're birds, as
if we can be tamed, caged. I'm
a human being.

Wondering

In the future, you
can do this, he said. Wait. Are
we in the future?

Working Mom, Exhibit A

He hands me a book.
There is work to do, so I
read with him instead.

Working Mom, Exhibit B

He wandered over
to my lap, and though I'm working
I let him stay.

See also: Time, Unproductive

World, How to Change the

Speak the words you want
to say with great kindness and
love. Heal the world whole.

See also: Responsibility

Worrying I

If one could tell my
mind to stop its worrying
I would be grateful.

Worrying II

I've gained something from
worrying; it's this: practiced

imagination.

See also: Anxiety, Exhibits A-F

Write

I am learning how
to bleed on a page for you
So be kind, reader

See also: Author; Know, How to

Writerly Persistence

What does a writer
do when a book launches, tanks?
Begin on the next.

| Life: a definition of terms |

Wrong, the Times I Am

I need a jacket.
You don't. It's summer. We walk
outside, into cold.

XO

I don't know which one
stands for hugs and which one stands
for kisses. Do you?

Yarn

He didn't do it,
he says, and spins round me a
fantastical tale.

Years

They say the days are
long but the years are short, and
I understand now.

Yes

If you asked me to
marry you all over again
I would say yes.

See also: Husband, Exhibits A-C; Husband, a Love Letter to My

Zoo

If life is like a
zoo, then I am a pleased,
contented zookeeper.

See also: Family, Home

Don't miss out on a poetry release! Visit www.racheltoalson.com/freebook to keep up-to-date on book and product releases and to access bonus material, including some free books.

About the Author

Rachel has studied the great art of poetry for more than a decade. She can be seen at least once a day pulling out her poetry notebook and jotting down some quick lines. Life, she says, is a grand poem, waiting to be recorded—which is why she never leaves home without her writer's notebook and a pen.

She is the author of *This is How You Know* and multiple poems for both adults and children that have been published in literary magazines and online publications around the world.

Rachel lives with her husband and six boys, who join her in a poetry slam session every Thursday afternoon, in San Antonio, Texas, where she faithfully writes at least a poem a day.

Author's Note

My dear reader,

It is my great hope that you have enjoyed reading this book immensely, just as I have enjoyed writing it immensely. I believe that when we stop and take notice of our world, as poetry demands that we do, we can see a deeper meaning to it all, whether that happens in relationships, in situations, or in personal stories of depression, anxiety, and joy. I try to capture each facet of living, however far removed they are from one another, because writing clarifies my world and records what I notice happening in it, in me, in all of us.

Poetry is a good way to remain present, and I hope the reading of my poetry has provided for you a way to remain present in your own world. When we stop and take notice of the small little details that become large in our attention, we can multiply our moments, stretch them, squeeze out of them every drop of meaning and ecstasy.

If you can think of anyone who needs this book and the encouragement and enlightenment that lives within it, please pass it along. Reader word of mouth is one of the greatest tools a writer has to share about her work.

Another valuable way to get this book into the hands of other readers is to leave a review wherever you bought it. It only takes a minute and a sentence or two, and it will be incalculably appreciated. (If you compose your review as a poem—whether haiku or otherwise—send me a screenshot at rachel@racheltoalson.com (include your address), and I'll send the first 25 who do it a paperback copy of the book.)

Thank you for your support.

In love,

Rachel

Acknowledgements

A book is never written in isolation, even though the bulk of my writing is done in my bedroom, with my door closed. This book would not have been possible without the following people:

My husband, who gave me the space to jot down a haiku every evening at 8 p.m. and who didn't say a word when I handed him my imperfect hand-lettering and asked him to scan it (because he's the technological genius around here, not me)

My kids, who gave me plenty of material from which to construct my poems

My brother, sister, mother, stepfather, stepbrother and all my brothers- and sisters-in-law, who show me, every day, what it means to disagree and still love each other

All the poets who have laid my poetry groundwork in their profound compositions

My readers, who make writing pleasurable

Thank you all.

Enjoy more poetry from Rachel Toalson

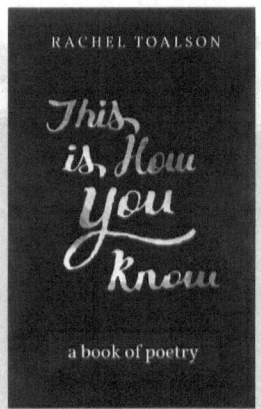
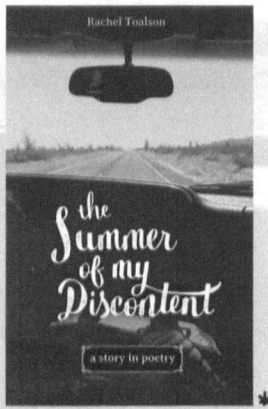

racheltoalson.com/poetry

available for free as a part of the poetry starter library

Rachel Toalson Poetry
Starter Library

Enjoy more of Rachel Toalson's poetry with these free downloads.

To get your FREE books, visit *
RachelToalson.com/FreeBook

*Must be 13 or older to be eligible

www.ingramcontent.com/pod-product-compliance
Lightning Source LLC
Chambersburg PA
CBHW021431080526
44588CB00009B/496